Heroics

Poems

by

Joanne Lowery

Avisson Press, Inc.
Greensboro

Heroics

Published by Avisson Press, Inc., P.O. Box 38816, Greensboro, North Carolina 27438 USA.

ISBN 1-888105-09-7
Library of Congress Catalog Card Number 96-84735

First Edition
Manufactured in the United States of America

With best wishes,
Joanne Lowery
January 1997

To R H

You want me to be sorry?
That fruit was like no other,
and I am his long missing rib.

Acknowledgments

"Van Eyck's Wings"	*New Letters*
"Van Eyck's View"	*New Letters*
"Nightmares"	*Aileron*
"Lapps"	*Aileron*
"Daughters"	*Maryland Poetry Review*
"Chaos"	*Aileron*
"Blue"	*Black River Review*
"Kierkegaard"	*Radix*
"Kierkegaard Writes to Ann Landers"	*Iowa Woman*
"Regine Schlegel in the Danish West Indies, January 1856"	*Iowa Woman*
"Eve"	*Mississippi Valley Review*
"Death of Simon Peter"	*Snake Nation Review*
"Don Juan Leaves the Coast"	*Soundings East*
"Slavery"	*Black River Review*
"Leningrad in Illinois"	*Spoon River Poetry Review*
"Stalingrad of the Midwest"	*Spoon River Poetry Review*
"Still Life: Woman with Pear"	*Spoon River Poetry Review*
"Still Life: Woman with Vase"	*Spoon River Poetry Review*
"Still Life: Woman with Body"	*Spoon River Poetry Review*

Table of Contents

Historic Voices

The Voyages of Captain James Cook

The Life of Carl Linnaeus

The Words of Fyodor Dostoevsky

The Experience of Søren Kierkegaard

The Paintings of Jan Van Eyck

The Memories of Guinevere

Still Lives

Historic Voices

Eve

It had rained that morning
so the Garden was white with mist
and rivulets trickled down my flanks.
When I heard hissing in the grass
I thought the earth was steaming
like a young star about to catch fire.
I never thought: serpent.
I never thought: sin.

And despite what they may tell you
Adam was not the first, but he was
the tallest of the men I came to favor
and could reach the red toy I fancied
from the wet tree. He turned it over
in his human hand and with a finger
felt the place the stem had entered.
I let him choose a name for it
while the snake in the grass applauded
like a joyful amputee.

Of course he ate it, and then he tasted me
under a dripping elderberry bush
where there was green stuff growing.
I remember so little about what changed everything.
Sometimes I think the sky was still blue
as he found me to his liking,
sometimes I think the tree became suddenly bare
and it was snow that forced us into clothes.
When I knelt down to set my eye
where the grass split apart from the snake's slither
I thought I saw in the shadowed cave
at the far end among clover and spears

a woman content to be unfed and alone.
But then his finger touched my shoulder
and I turned to where he lay,
a bit of white flesh still caught in his teeth.
You want me to be sorry?
That fruit was like no other,
and I am his long missing rib.

Lazarus Listens to the Frogs

Now that I am about to die a second time
into the long sleep of glory,
I leave to my sisters
a vision of spring's ripe light
spilling through linen bands:
the cave and rock behind me,
a friend's heavenly face,
the crowd stepping back
as if four days hadn't happened.

Forgive my complaint at brightness
and the injustice that I alone
was called back to life.
What I first heard
was not the resurrector's own surprise
or the gasp among his doubtful
but how the fallen cloth
hushed a fold of grass
where I found myself standing.
Morning dried the muddy heads of angels
down the hill, bloated pipes of song.
Mary and Martha, remember to love
the body. Remember that I raised a hand
to touch my distant throat
and wanted to hear more.

Death of Simon Peter

Years later, when they hung him upside down
to mirror-image-mock all he had been saying
about the friend who called him rock
and gave him a church to martyr for,
he had the time, head full of gravity and blood,
to watch his feet be wiped dry
by clouds. It was just before sunset,
right before his unrecorded death
that fellowship came to him, too late
as it always will, despite the iron rod of anger
that makes cowards of us all.
Who was he to protest the humble washing
of his dust-bitten feet? They spun
a ball of fire moments before his end.
It was a miracle that he even walked
or wanted to be clean or understood
after years of staring at nets
and wanting their heaviness to pull at his arms
the word free. The fish had been
so helpless in their dry wiggling.
But hands are split even finer
into fingers that brace the precious bowl.
It felt so good, skin and water,
touch and the air that breathed
upon his toes release.
His last word was marvelous.

Coronado Climbs the Same Old Mountain

and sits on a rock
in the Spanish shadow of despair.

It is another morning of the endless search
for seven fabled cities.
Kindly have the kindness not to tell him
that the only towns he will find
are filled with clay people
poor in metals, rich in

views of a slanted world
studded with green statues,
cholla, pinōn, aspen
and all the unnamed

flowering things adorning this cage of birds.
Here is the pinnacle of all sunshine,
the cliff of a changing moon.
Listen to the clatter of streams
falling to the equator.

You are a mile high and do not know it.
Sea level covers all your years.

The rocks gathered around his boots
are sharp and polished with tongues:

Let the dead sing their praises.
Or let him take them back
in the bellies of ships
to be the stuff of palaces
for viceroys and tourists.

Then the land will discover tiny places
to grow, without him, grow
mountains clouded in treasure.
For the last years of his life

he leads an expedition north
to desire's magnetic center.
Behold dry eden and him,
an eagle abreast of thin air.
At the altitude of angels
a senorita lies ready to surrender.

Don Juan Leaves the Coast

and the jungles and the mountains come alive,
small birds twitter.

An inland waterfall carries his sweat
over rocks and past ferns

where the news of his passing swings a vine for monkeys
he fed from the palm of his hand.

Finally his brow is dry enough for garlands
to shield his tropical eyes

and his shoulders consent to bear
the cape of parakeet feathers sewn by

passionate women.
The mountains and the valleys stay full

of black-haired beauties who open like orchids
at the thought of his touch.

Don't leave us, the verdant hills echo
as he heads for the empty beach.

Does he hear them, does he lay down his pack
on the damp sand?

This is the new edge of his rich rich life
where he stands munching on fruit

and scanning the waves for sails
as the ocean scallops the sky.

The only flesh he feels is his own
while from the distant trees parrots
break their promises.

13

Slavery

Come morning the sound of the clapper,
                    the sound of crows.
Who told night it could disappear?

I step over the smoky lumps of children
who once were me
to find the door.
The wide wide world stands open-armed,
but I am legless to go walking

except to the Big House
where I comb her sticky long hair.
She tells me I am too dumb for French braiding,
she tells me to fan the noonday sun,
she tells me recollect recollect recollect
                    I turn my head crying.

There is no place to run to
though the children duck beneath the fence
and back over the top rail whooping
loud enough to scare the early moon,

loud enough to bring her coming round the porch
with her yellow smile, the mad twitch,
her stumbling over the name she once chose
as she beckons me with the branch of her finger,
shadow of a free tree.
I bob without a word
                    chained to silence.

Mary Lincoln: Bellevue Place, 1875

1

Even the name is a sham,
as if there were a beautiful view from this window
to calm the temperament of those of us
kept here like crazy ladies.
Through the new-leafed trees I only see
that ditch of a river, the Fox.

2

Even my name is a sham,
that anyone born of me should be blessed
whereas a heap of dead little boys
is all I have to show
for what I bore the President.
And Robert, who had me sent here,
for the sake of my money.

3

All day I hear the clang of picks
as they break apart limestone in the quarry
across the avenue by the water's edge.
My complaints have done nothing
but scatter the crows that cry
and fold their wings against heaven.

4

He freed the slaves but not me.
Their anthracite eyes withheld the glint of gratitude,
whereas I would be most beholding
if he came back to lift the veil of widowhood
from my naked face.

5

Perhaps he lies in the arms of his Ann
who remains sprinkled with malarial dew.
They joke about what he did with me
until her dead cheeks blush.
I am imprisoned by a woman's shame.

6

Although they are kind to me here,
it is not enough for a lifetime

wrapped in ragged shawls.
What have I done except loved
and written letters?

7

This town watches me stroll the grounds
of my allotted freedom: a madwoman
with a famous name and combed hair.
Where they have taken my life I now leave
my name as a marker of female agony
for generations of women to come.
May they stay sane and unmarried.

Leningrad in Illinois

This same three-colored view
from different windows:
blue, white, and hunger.

I go out to squash stars
beneath my skis along the river.
Each tree is limned with chalk

but it's sugar I want,
sticky from animal heat
as the body forages.

I know what lies buried in snow—
the decadence of our past
and a longing for new bread

come to me from the Ukraine.
If I saw someone slumped against a tree
I would pivot in a snowy spray

startling the mourning doves
to settle on his gray shoulders.
His bare hand makes tracks of beckoning

toward the Neva's share of ice and danger,
but survival is a sport the dead can't play.
Otherwise I would lie down too,

this little self denting feathers.
The blue I see is my own eyes
bright with starvation.
The white is the long wait,
the sweet world,
someone staring at the sky.

Stalingrad of the Midwest

A basin of land, a great river.
And a cold city come morning

the rubble of fallen branches bathed
in soupish light,
bushes like mushrooms of monstrous feasting,
their bloodless stalks preserved by snow.

A girl stands listening on the shore
while the boatman drags his life
with rope and song.
Inside her lives the *babushka* of old age
inside her lives the pearl of her daughter's grace
inside her lives descendants so small
that everything she does will be forgotten.
He smiles, ready to pare her
peel by peel to her unknown core.

At least they will be warm together
among ruins, the sun's fire too far
to thaw solitary skin.
He has resolved to defend their motherland
if blue-eyed strangers converge
with purple guns.
Even together cold beasts bite their fingers,
yet that is the way it has always been:

waking to a war we never expect
and young love over
we reach for beauty's bright scarf.
How else can victors explain the red bloom
frozen on these wooden mouths?

Taiga and Plains

Colorblind in the winter forest
numbed by cross-hatched shadows
I long for a different cheek of globe.

But purple is all I find
cracking porcelain snow
brandy wasted on sky
domino tracks unique to each hare's passing.

My own lay a crooked path
of left and right hollows.
Over the next white hill
stretches world without end
no women, zero men.

East to west the transcontinental line
shakes muffled castanets
all for the hum of revolution.
While in the royal car, red velvet worn bare,
a crone strokes her spinning wheel
into silver hoops of prairie.

An unbeliever pokes holes with his knobby stick
then asks about lavender and tea.
He understands this is a cold time.
I show him an empty coat
cooling its ghost on the checkered ground.

Let me explain the small silky space
between wool and body.
Something you cannot see lives there
smelling familiar,
an invisible lining for your heart.
Believe in it, call it a blessing.

The Voyages of Captain James Cook

Captain James Cook Contemplates
Comparison with Jonah

Tonight as the ship shivers through
a mountainous week-long storm
I envy Jonah his three belly-bound days
warm, or at least sheltered
from elements scarcely pacific.
If he strung a hammock rib to rib
he'd sway in unison with the natural journey
of a great fish.
          While this less than great ship,
a refurbished collier, the *Endeavor* tries to be
for me and my men a kind of land,
a firmament that takes us God knows where
I decide. I can't blame him for turning away
from Ninevah and the Lord's command.
The ocean begs us to disobey everything
except the kiss of blue-on-blue horizon.

Still, as I slam against the cabin wall
in need of sleep and as offensive
to Hygeia as he was in undigested stink
with no way to relieve this body
of its unwelcome love of comfort,
I do not long for Yorkshire fields
as a place to perish, the same hills
limned on my eyes day after day
adventureless, an ordinary sinking
with no hope of being spewed forth
come morning to calm water and sun.
Here where no fish would want us
we agree to endure the promise of God:
All this I gave you.

Captain James Cook
Overtakes A Dream

From time to time
I spend hours
fore, near the prow,
my gaze transfixed
on the same but changing
space between two waves,

profundus: water to a depth
that man exists no more.
Life is a little something
bobbing along the top.

What if in that galaxy of ocean
we find another life,
another sort of man,
the noble savage amidst plenty
where answers grow like breadfruit
and a tangle of emerald valleys
defines the good and beautiful.

There everyone cultivates emotion
untainted by memory or mood.
With warm fingers
she feeds me bits of fish
and sweet potato, shares
a wrap of rough fabric.
When Banks sees her
he creates a new name.

Oh innocent day — dawn of
utopian temperatures and plain needs,
ease alternating with pleasure.
Let simplicity reign.
With white teeth and proffered hand
we dance around their fire.
None of this whip, tuppence,

complicated cargo.

Light breezes will render
all calculation pointless.
Content, we will stay
to grow old and fearless,
climb the fogged peak
that has sustained us
and through a blue gap

see a flagged bird
find the bay
and lay those curious eggs
from which emerge
metal, mirror, and French disease.

A sudden sousing spray.
I wipe my eyes on this navy sleeve,
look up as the cry goes out:
Tahiti.

Reef

Let me tell you about danger,
how it is everywhere,
the export of Hades and below.

A ship is like a seed on a lake.
But even a seed has a bottom
and water is readily displaced.

In 1770 Cook sailed the *Endeavor*
northward inside Australia's unexplored
east coast phenomenon, the Great Barrier Reef.

He named everything that stood in his way,
he mapped each proven passage
where islands, shoals and cays
rose and fell among the crashing water.

Coral everywhere told him stop,
grazing the tender hull,
piercing wood with limestone rock
to let black water pour in.

Staunching the hole, navigating
in and out between land, reef and sea
he took note of beauty:
green valleys, lizards, coral sculpture,
the broad rainbow of blues

in a place where luck was a changing tide
of things as they were, things as they are.
He was no coward, no quailing dummy.
He walked the plank to look ahead
calculating ebb versus wind,
current among shallows.

Neptune blessed the clever ship
with a gap deep enough for passing through.

New Guinea separated itself from Cape York
and Cook sailed safely into open sea.

Because he was not dead
he could tell the world what the reef permits
between Cape Townsend and Torres Strait,
how he and his crew survived
a gauntlet of superlatives.

How what kept them going
for twelve hundred perilous miles
was the will of a brilliant fool.

Captain James Cook Hears Jimmy Corcoran
Aboard the *Resolution*
Approaching the Antarctic Circle
At Midnight, 16 January 1773

My crew think I know what I am doing
exploring every ocean, a son of God
out to disprove Dalrymple's fabled land
which by this twenty-hour light
they can see is myth melting.

Kendall's chronometer got us here,
and my resolve. Now, gales abated,
stillness makes me ache
to come on deck where a few hands
steer us among a range
of floating pastel mountains
Tahitian pink to paradise green,
a sight so shimmering
it salts my eyes.
Stiff canvas, iron rope, glazed timbers
hold.

His watch relieved, the Irish lad
press-ganged to our service, so he says,
Corcoran follows me to the rail.
        Aye, Sir, our sister ships
as the bergs cluster, glide past

and though I've heard him sing before,
an instrument of grace, his tenor
this late, this cold, this far stirs me.
        The world goes on forever
        This world is all we know
while the hull hisses and crunches
us to the bottom of the globe,
his voice a gull over black water.
        We can't go on forever

We are small we know

Having seen these cliffs of ice
white as the thighs of a woman
we will return to England
circumscribed as islands.
       Call me Jimmy
       Call me Jesus
       Call me Captain Echo
I who have named places
Plenty, Tribulation, and Sorrow
travel a perpetual Sea of Marvel.

So it goes: an expanse of feathered heaven
or undulating hell.
Meanwhile his song unspools and sails
ahead to disappear like beauty
while a thousand ice floes separate us
from fame and plumage,
fronds and pure music.
       A man can only wonder
       Where the wind will blow

 Resolution noses the next crevasse,
passage farther or journey back
to the beach where tropical princes
beg the sun for our return.
I lean toward their drums,
hum Jimmy's ditty,
fill the crew's bellies
with sauerkraut and imagination.

Elizabeth Cook Recalls the Captain's
Last Leavetaking

The night before I sat by the hearth
mending his stockings.
The bloom's still on you, Liz-o.
I nodded rather than blame the fire,
and perhaps there were still coals of desire

for the man who came and went
those thirteen years, leaving souvenirs
all of whom died except the two eldest boys
who later went to their father's sea.
Never love a man who tries to walk on water.

He had such a pure-sky eye
lit with the sum of all his knowing
unfathomable to us all, even the men
who shared his ship, who watched
his watching the world.

When tales flew about Tahitian women
with their open brown treasures,
I wondered. I knew what he liked.
I knew I was simple and smelled like bread

while he was wet wool, brine and hemp
filling my arms as I stood on the Thames,
then waving. Already he was giving orders,
cloudless eyes mast to rail.

I became a famous widow for the same reason
he wed me: it had to be someone.
So Elizabeth Batts and our babies became his
for a time, his fleshly islands and shore.

After he left in search of the Northwest Passage
I lived the rest of my life
discovering the word never.

The Apotheosis of Captain Cook

What we discover gets us in the end.

Sailing along, for once unsuspecting,
the great explorer came upon one last batch
of islands, pronounced them Sandwich.

Again canoes came alongside.
Small dark people were in need of a god.
What to trade, what to trade?

On his return visit, early 1778,
they proved his head could be bashed
with volcanic stone.
Every god must die a first death.

In Kealakekua Bay a small fish
swam past his reluctant face.
With red feathers waving
the chiefs carried their prize shell
to the beach, stripped its meat,
handed out pearly bones to the faithful.

Here are his skull and gun
to set upon your table.
He was spared the sight of his own demise,
still stunned by miscalculation and power,
wondering how he came to rest on clouds
looking downward.
None of the angels obeyed him,
their wings stiff and windless.

Welcome to Paradise, they said.
Eternity begins
now that you changed the world.

The Life of Carl Linnaeus

Nightmares

The boy Carl sleeps in Sweden's winter.
His mind becomes a leaf
blown from home and temple
into the savage world.

There can be no going back
to the life of the seed:
he has begun to view creation
in all its unnamed parts

in all its unknown shadows.
Stamens beckon.
All the petals, as he has guessed,
lie open.

God, wigged with clouds,
confuses earth's various grandeur.
Weeds everywhere. Thistles.
Beaks of birds prying.

He dreams he is lost in a garden
where everything grows the same.

Lapps

When the rye and birch began greening
Linné set out to inventory
a land of never-ending sun.

Wearing tree bark they greeted him,
shared raw fish and smoked tongue,
sat naked in their huts
so he could watch them wither.

He survived bogs, midges, magic,
and a shrub beautiful as Andromeda.

During long nights he saw everything
as a scientist. A priest said

> The clouds are solid
> and sweep us away like lemmings.
>
> We grow back:
> deer rough as lichen,
> people smooth as moss.

Drink our milk,
you will want to return
for its human taste.

Friends

Lost in Amsterdam
Peter Artedi studied ichthyology

what to do with all those fish
that fed upon my plants.

A genius missed his way
stupidly drowning in a canal
one night on his way home.

In exchange for names and places
the least they could have done
was teach him breath and fin.

The circle closed to a bubble
beneath an arched bridge.
For two more days before the news came

I thought I had a friend
with whom to divide the world.
Peter, I would say,

what about mermaids,
drowned sailors, young men?

Daughters

If you sow four seeds
from my *Linnaea borealis*
you'll get four of the same

but from my wife
four odd girls sprang.
Only a nose, a quirk
traces their lineage

though the little sweet one
used to help me tend my flowers.
Mostly they have grown

bosoms and the need for more
with the inclination to nag
like their uninspired mother.
It was not my interest

to produce from myself perfection
when I took her to me,
but yes, yes

I expected familiar faces,
discipleship, better nature,
a legacy of slender girth.

Lisa, Lovisa, Sara and Sophia,
have you read my wonderful books?

Flowers

It is a fine day.

Welcome to my Garden
where three thousand species
do the work of the Sun.

We have clipped the hedge
low and regular,
a geometric Maze

against which the flowers
perform their bouquet.

Those pink lilies you admire
are *Lycoris radiata*,
a hardy amaryllis
shaded by *Arbor vitae*.

In early summer
they lose their leaves,
and green fades from their stems
colored broth and tentacle.

Think of all the Bulb knows
releasing its spears,
faith in the furled flag
soon to become Corolla.

Count the petals and knobbed stamens,
the flowers jointed to a single stem
where pink hints lavender
and streaks of sunset gold.

Imagine hundreds of pastel clouds
trumpeting the coming Storm.

You can see where birds and bees go,
where the butterfly hangs like a leaf.
When Winter seeds your window with snow

remember that we planted them
in neat graveyard rows.
Already some twist brown Fingers.

Jealousy: their pale Flesh will nod again.

Delights

Everywhere
The white wings of Alpine ptarmigans
Summer lightning
How the membrane in grasshopper wings vibrates for
sound
An elephant embryo, preserved
Saxifraga stellaris and its name
Growing bananas in Uppsala, Sweden
Enough memory for 5,900 binomial species
Harmony
The gift of a carved rhino-horn cup from China
To have lived more years than one's father
The free love of flowers
Women
Deus creavit, Linnaeus disposuit
Infinity

Chaos

Old men like to think of order—
minuets and even stitches,
snowflakes and orbits,
boxes each with a label.

Those wild boys keep tearing up the path
we groomed for them
through endless forest.

Earth, dear sphere, our desire to know
our desire to live
complicates you
with roots and jungle.

The surface of life is glass
except for emotions.
Creator, take from us this cup of feelings.

It is time to trade the body
for a spiderweb's starburst symmetry.
We walk into silver light,
pull it from our faces.

The Words of Fyodor Dostoevsky

Survival

Every mother is a stick
and Russia a whole forest

mostly bare, the sticks having split
for sons who go to war
or disappear due to state,
mothers wailing.

She named me Fyodor for her father,
a man unlike my own
who spat at her virtue,
half of me born of a drunken worm.

I remember her finger on this cheek
pointing to a rose.
Then she'd laugh
and go tend the baby.

Then she'd cough
a red star on her bed.
I went outside to watch
constellations of women light the sky.

Then picked up an axe
and walloped at what lay fallen.
Mother Russia, are you glad you outlived
one boy's bitter story?

Silence

Not the sound of our feet on our last December morning
Not the name Fyodor Dostoevsky among others
Not our shared firing squad sentence: So be it
Not the crisp paper refolded by a cold hand
Not the woodpecker song of a dozen drums
Not the ritual cracking of swords across our heads

as we kneeled
as the priest held out the cross
as our lips grazed it with sin and vapor
as we looked our last looking into the sky
as we felt with our last feeling one body's space
as our minds tried to imagine the impossible leap

when my three friends were tied hooded to three stakes
when sixteen ramrods clanged to be loaded
when we waited their turn while waiting our own
when we continued and the wind kept blowing
when the horse pounded louder than our blood
when we understood the words of imperial commutation

I cocked my head, shook it,
began to hear something else, a black ringing
the rest of my life.

Siberia

Europe's morning is tea and nectar
in the eastern sky.
Buried past Urals
we wake in the barracks
to begin this day
gray masks before gray faces.

As I fill my hod with bricks
our dawn lightens
clear as some tropical bay.
Such colors amid snow scrunching
with cold worse than cutting knives,
certainly one iron spike
cornered in my left eye.
I must not rub at weeping.

I try the trick for desperate fools:
shut off all sense of feeling
and become creature of pure sight.
No hunger, no heavy load,
no pain nor freezing penetrates
this numb body.

I watch the woman I will love
dress beside the fire.

I watch a certain hero's heart
slowly change past doubt.

I watch my hand remove its glove
to begin writing.

I know what men smell like,
I can taste the cracked lip's sap.
Bricks pile higher.

Only one more year.

Blue

A January sun turns the open snow to blue,
paths of trees and falling walls laid upon the ground.
Dostoevsky's heir would rather write a page on beauty
than contemplate what might happen next
to the bruise mottling his left shin.
Soon this day will end in a victory of shadows
except for ghosts from breath and moon.
A man in love with his blanket is afraid
the whole night will become the pain in his leg.
Cold morning will tell if that is true.

Fate

The wheel is iron
heavy as an old serf's cart
stained with Stenka Razin's blood.

So it rolls day after day
crushing us
in life's downhill spin.

The gambler prefers wire, wood and air
blurred by a clever finger
outfoxing the common fox
pushing dullness to the brink.

Something will happen, nothing stays sane.
If I pawn our wedding bands
and Anna's only warm coat
if I wager my very mind
life will turn topsy-turvy.
Clickety-clickety, roll of the dice.
Win or lose, I did it.

One day I stopped,
let my pen rule others instead.
We slowly rose out of debt
into volumes of passion and sainthood,
envy, parricide and ruin.

I named them Raskolnikov, Alyosha, Myshkin,
let their last page come full circle.

Seizure

I become a wolf, the wolf adores me.

Full moon on a rainy night,
a howling from the golden dome.

I have gone where you will never go.
The body looks like what it is,
meat for the twisted beast

while I live five seconds or forever.
Memories of the future
pour from Zeus' bolt.

Last time surely I saw heaven:
ten thousand silver words
scattered by His hand,
a storm of truth,
beauty understood.

Then the slow cave,
our Slavic world.
My head aches,
the wolf licks
sad Anna's sad face.

Sin

Murder of course is the best,
the candle held to all others.

A saint loves to kill
practicing on hares and children,
the self, Jesus and Satan.

I did it, he smiles, freshly human.
Now try to understand.

Life is a little sliver I sliced
from someone's ox-like heart.
He is too dead to miss it.

All my life I have wanted
to hold my hand to the heat,
pinch spit on a pure flame.

Soul

This is our parade through the ice storm forest.
Chaff falls from a white sky,
birches rattle.
The path goes on and on.

Dostoevsky sips his tea, creates a man:
frozen beard, crimson heart, slow stride slipping
page to page.

Where dumb beasts leave their prints
his felt-bound hero's feet
pause in ragged holes.
From a prismed branch
one bird sings.

His man must feel everything
dragging an intersection of sticks
across the desert, the taiga, the sea.
And so he remembers his life,
strokes his eternal cheek,
imagines another chance.

When the writer quit his crooked lines
Karamazov argued for afterlife.
God loves this world without him.
So we suffer, we suffer and hope.

The Experience of Søren Kierkegaard

Søren's Solstice

He was one small tree
on Jutland's shore
stunted in the winter light.

Everyone else lived on the equator
where the land was yellow
the fruit dazzling
the ocean endless bath
and days equaled their duration.

Instead on earth's pointy forehead
his hands grabbed at darkness
more slippery than the fateful circumstances
of his loveless birth.
Danishly he lived thinking

he needed light to see
the state of men and nations
to illumine love's black heart
to walk to the fish market whistling.

What we want gets denied us.
Afternoon becomes late morning.
Candles lose their tall ends.

We say to him a hundred-plus years later
it was for the greater good
you learned the texture of despair

how God's cheek feels mid-December
how weakly morning waits to see
if your wits succeeded seeking
midnight's perfect center.

Now we know despair is winter's friend
making blind beggars of us all.
Toward the end when he knew
only one black star would follow

the orbit of things became almost pleasing.
So it is dark.
So nothing grows.
What he touched stays invisible.

S. K.'s Legacy

Such a little thing:
as a boy my father gnawed
God's love till in his hunger
he cursed Life Divine.
It was a childish blot

on the moment's need.
Later he saw with melancholy clarity
how easily the blessed lose
every beatitude: wives, children,
fortune and blood.

He became a kind of fierce sun
risen outside my daily window.
I sit at my desk and try to shade
the constellation of guilty griefs
he shines and shines and shines on me.

See the arched shadow on the flat wall.
So be it, crooked body with a polar soul
of his old sad making.
Father, I never had to ask
if you remember the thoughtless night
you raised her gown to give me

this lifetime of unrelieved dread.
Knowing me now, you would do it again
for the sake of experience and books
and call it sire's love.
But I know differently
and elect to doom our family tree.

God Himself chose to suffer only one Son.
You tried for more, I cannot fault you.
But I know differently.
On the wall behind us I become
a fair rendition of starvation's sowing.

Kierkegaard

Less than famous, scarcely known
the Dane banished his queen,
took on the guilt of fathers,
and promised to explain
our Christian bliss.

Who among us shall have the luck to wed?
He stayed a boy.
He chased words.
His flesh became despair.

Father, I have sinned
and therefore am entitled to be happy.
My name on books
my name on children
or her sweet face across the table
will not drive me from this pulpit
where only You can hear me speak
and see my small heart smile.
I live as if faith heals me.

Kierkegaard Writes to Ann Landers

Dear Ann
I read with interest your reply
to the moody Dane who left his love
floating on water.

Not everyone is a prince
but I can monologue
even more than he
if not so eloquently
if not for an audience
like yours in the millions.

Like him I spurned a lady
and lost her to regret.
If the truth be known
if I be so brave as tell a stranger
I admit: I obsess.

Don't tell me to confess
to clergy. They are ignorant.

Or get help from a doctor.
Study doesn't make men wise.

Nor suggest exercise
in this damp Baltic air.
I am the famous cripple
who walks crooked streets everywhere.

Instead

tell me how to bridge
the exquisite space
between man and woman
between body and soul

how at the next salon

to use my wit
to make the host human

by what means of living and writing
I can convince God
we shouldn't need this yoke
to pull from Him some answer.

If the woman I love writes to you
I will be elsewhere, busy
making a diamond out of morning.

From now on I will fold the paper
to avoid your column's page.
Because I know what I would read
in bold ink, what I saw in Regine's eyes,
what makes my friends turn away.

Ann, I am happy how I suffer.
All I want is permission,
say you understand.

Regine Schlegel in the Danish West Indies,
January 1856

This morning I climbed the hill
behind the Governor's Palace where Fritz and I live
to supervise the trimming of the graveyard
as we begin the new year.

There in the *kirkegaard* where canecutters
and rebels blacken the earth
I feel myself exposed to the blue eye
of heaven and the cloudless twinkle
of that thinker who saw me as his own,
the news having just arrived
that he died as winter was commencing.

That he died, that life left Søren
seems impossible. Fritz's small safe smile.

When I was a girl he made of me
such a goddess, such a queen
I prayed to match him.
But I couldn't and so my being
added to the dark side of his moon.
Now at least God illumines him

while I say well done
to the gardener and his crew.
The dead lie in their places.
And the churchyard holds
what's left of love.

Despite the breeze on the verandah
I long to retire to my room
where I can see the eastern shore.
I untie the apron streaked
with scythed grasses.
I untie the skirt, the overslip,
the petticoat, every muslin layer

between the world and my stays.
I unlace myself from the day.

Then the camisole in exchange
for a billowing cotton gown.
My hands fumble the knot of memory.
What he wanted I could not give—
no matter, his wanting bound us.
Praise God I still remember
his words, his face rippling with grief.
Praise God who sets the little man free.

S. K.'s Flying Carpet

is woven from pewter thread
with iron woof and fringe

flies into Hegel's ear
on the way from Copenhagen
to Berlin and back again

zooms among the global heirs
of a Nordic philosophic pioneer

who sat astride a bed of nails
to levitate and squint
at elusive destinations:

the speed of life bore him
poet thinker sinner
forty-two years above common ground.

Startled from spires
Denmark's doves stared.
How close to God
can a smart man get?

These souvenirs: a hunched pilot
existential wreckage
his rug to warm our feet.

S. K.: Reflection

There are no answers.

But questions flourish
blessing us
with their interrogative beauty.

God gave me a key
to unlock my mouth
to stick in my ear
to twirl before my eyes
to furrow across my brow
words without ceasing.

Yet I am reticent
compared to Felix
who lives downstairs
caretaker of us all.
When he sweeps the stairs

he greets each mote of dust
like a fond child
apologizing for the necessary heap.
Lovely day, Herre K,
he says when it is raining.
I did a fine job of shooing
the rats by the back door,
don't you think, Herre K,
don't you think?

How God must love
his human heart
while I compete with angels.

If I were not blinded
by love of the Father
I would see only a world
staring dumbly back.

Like simple Felix
I would keep the corners clean,
enjoy fresh bread,
forget my mockers and Regine.

Instead I watch wave after wave
of endless gray water
scallop the beach.
Each drop bursts into word.
Surely in this short life
in the miles my legs
have one-two one-two borne me
I shall come upon that single flash
that pinch that explains everything.

I live: hold one word to my eye
like glass, turn it to examine
light inner/light outer.
And die: awash in divine color.

The Paintings of Jan Van Eyck

Van Eyck's Wings

From the beamed corner she beckons—
bent finger, straight nose, heavy eyes
as if she means to bestow her stalk
of lilies to us as clapperless bells.

What news does she know that we don't?
What truth beneath cleric's robes
is all eternity keeping?

If we step closer we may hear
the linen crescendo of her saffron cape,
smell mustiness from wall-bound mice,
feel the cold exhale of her hair.

Stuck to her back as an afterthought of locomotion
her wings perk into enormous ears
lined with scaling rows, each scallop
outlined in buttery hues, the rim
an unripened cartilage luminous green
with every feather salmon, melon, amber,
cucumber, spotted fawn, daffodil
and colors only God's own see.

If we step closer we may feel
their barbed tips grace us
with the mystery of world greeting air.
And if they fold into bottomless cups
our incredulous eyes may weep.

For five centuries we have breathed
turpentine and anticipation.

Van Eyck's Music

To hear them we must go to St. Bavon's
and listen to the altarpiece
where two brothers painted brocaded angels
gathered in song.

Their throats are full as they listen
to what we think we hear
but their eyes seem blank, blind
to sisterly sirensong.

Others use harp, pipes and strings:
words are never enough.
None of them looks happy
despite the right pitch, despite perfection.

When Hubert, the fabled elder, died
they took his painterly arm
and buried it there in the cathedral,

this because his use of tempera and glaze
they judged miraculous.
The ulna was just right for a baton.
Jan took it and kept them singing.

Van Eyck's View

Outside the world is Ghent.
A barnswallow tips past the cathedral.
It is always late afternoon

the shining dove divided into energetic wires
to sustain everything.
At the Second Coming there will no longer be shadow.

Until then we have windows without glass
so that his air brings orange blossom and rose
from as far away as Apocalypse.
There the Sacred Lamb waits upon the altar
envied by straight-haired sinners.

Gazing upon glory we separate out
into apostles, priests, burghers and wives
all choosing the same center panel.

Their faces look Flemish to a fault, surrounded
by grass green enough to be real.
They know life will never be sufficient,
mere trickling fountain where the dead converge.

Jan has not yet returned to update paradise:
the lamb remains radiant among his few
in a scene unchanged, a vision
human and angelic, perhaps divine.
From distant times we join his pilgrims
in unseen adoration.

Van Eyck's Pair

Their four hands float across the middle
of a 30 by 20 portrait, little John Arnolfini
and his petite wife, his right raised
as if to listen, the left in open clasp
of her right while her other blesses
her burgeoning belly

verdant green as his beaver hat
and the tassels hung on the bedroom wall.
Together they have been comfortable there.

Light comes from a side window, the candelabrum
and the eyes of their weird woolly dog.
John is vigilant, she waits.

Though they may gaze indirect
touch says it all.
He has attended to her needs,
her eyes are not sorry.
A wimple frames madonna's face

while the round mirror behind
holds a family in its sphere.
Above in Latin the artist's name, 1434.
We see their figures there, another mirror.
They are content to go on and on.

Van Eyck's Saint

lives, like us, on rocky ground,
and when stigmata appear
to show him how slowly life drains
Francis seems surprised, as we would be,
on his knees, the painter's perfect hands flowing.

His Assisi is a world of flowers on the cliff
and scrub tree from the crag,
birds unspoiled by what drifts above the town
what oozes from palm and sole
what hangs on a winged crucifix
to remind us of someone else's suffering.

Brother Leo dozes slumped beside miracle:
so the anonymous unchosen dream of heaven
as earthly wind whistles through orifices
no one, least of all Francis, understands.
He accepts what he sees, believing himself
the fool, the genius, a dabbler
in the mystery of flesh.
To convince us of holiness
he mixes just the right red.

The Memories of Guinevere

Guinevere Remembers the Tournament

Already they call this mere convention.
Last night I dreamed in the future
and pitied this self's dark age.

At noon the horn sounded, we rose
into the high sun, casting shadows
straight down upon ourselves.
I was all skirt, a dunce's hat
and cloud of lace

while L, my heart's liege
bore the burning suit of metal
that kept him uncloven
by tools of war.
He rode past, a clanky statue,

though I knew he was baby flesh
pink and white petal-sweet
one handful at a time.

I would peel the visor, the beaver,
the gorget, the breastplate, the tasse,
the cuisse, the kneepiece and greave
from the man I love,

applaud the sun upon his shoulders.
Let the crowd hush, his foe disappear.
Our king is mere evidence of marriage.
His horse bears a tin prisoner
through bloodless grass past the rail.
Like a deity the falcon scatters royal doves.

The field is empty, my hands emptier still.
Arthur coughs as I pull a vermilion scarf
from my sleeve, fumble, watch it fly.

Guinevere Remembers May

Everything, all you heard about
happened in spring. Always
the world was green abundance
while we in our youth
betrayed betrayed betrayed.
Perhaps it was all that rain

dripping through the impossible forest,
rivers full of themselves,
mists drifting against the current.

Rising those mornings I stood
at my private window
and watched the meadow thicken.
The scent of apple blossoms
entwined itself in my hair.

We would meet by the river
and nest among rooks and cranes.
The wet grass dragged at my cape
as he pulled me to my knees.

I complain to the priest
who weekly hears my confession
how long December lasts
albeit we wait for His coming.
Head shaved, eyelashes stiff with snow
I count endless penitential beads.
Things fall past the window:
snow, blossoms, teardrops, silver rain.

When I finish repeating endless sins,
hurrying so he can return to the fire,
I tell him what he is too young to know.

There is no need to mortify the flesh,
so surely it mortifies itself in time.

Guinevere Remembers Her Cape

I was just a girl chosen by the King.
Then they made a work of art
in which to hide their unripe queen
and call her beautiful.

Crimson brocade embroidered
with peacocks from another realm
draped these royal shoulders,
a cape lined in soft fog
and buttoned with blazing copper
lit by golden thread and shiny black stones,
a kingdom rustling at their gasp

as I stately did proceed to join him
on the throne. Inside
I shivered, clutched its thick walls
until my body's heat spun a cocoon
in which to dream wings
that bore me over the countryside:
small white sheep, cattle, peasants
in their created places.

When I came to Almesbury
they kept it at the gate to return
empty of woman, cold silk.
Next time I die I will leave nothing,
no souvenir shell recognized
by genius, goodness, or the gallant.
Oh this dear nakedness.
Above the collar the same smile
wears thin a little longer.

Guinevere Remembers the Fair

When we rode down the hill to join them
the crowd parted like wings on a swan.
Hail, our King and his Queen.

Lancelot was already there,
feet propped on the lap of a maid
I knew he didn't love.
A juggler kept three red balls
and a flaming torch circling in air.

I followed a thread of smoke
to the edge of merriment
where hare and venison roasted.
An old woman turned the spit
while a child rubbed her shoulders.
The crone stopped humming,
stabbed a piece and held it forth
in a rag. It was for me
to empty her hand.

I left a penny on her blackened palm.
Each of us asked God to bless the other
and looked away.
The meat crusted with ash

I taste still, licking the bitterness
we need to keep this body alive.
Then there was music and dance
and the energy of forgetting
before night came to the green.
When I went back for another piece of meat
she was gone.

These hands at the rail
are withered with lack.
I bite my tongue to not ask
for one more celebration.

Guinevere Remembers Wanting It All

In this life I see dawn through a veil
as matins rings three, then four
and I lead them down the hall to pray

when all I want is sleep
even in my narrow bed.
I shake my shaved head amazed
that I once took the King and his knight
into the great chambers of my heart

and like some bird blown from France
on two gigantic wings
defied the world
to glide and keep gliding.

Now I have neither
nor child
nor green velvet dress.
This morning I yearn for sunset.

My prayers are for forgiveness.
Not L's, who never knew rue.
Oh, those were good times.
The King magnanimously understands.
But the world

which begrudged me word by word
is not ready to forgive
my hearts' desire, forever mine,
to never choose.

Guinevere Remembers Disappointment

I learned to lose at my mother's knee
when she told me the baby
had gone to live with God,
and then the next child too.
No, I cried, the morning her maid screamed
our lady had grown cold,

again when my father failed
to return from the hunt
and on my wedding night.
I saw another version set my lover's face
as he told me story after story
of not finding the Grail.
Yet then he'd turn and smile.

If the fields needed rain
our skies stayed blue.
The summer of floods
I woke every morning
to the certainty of more.
Soon nothing surprised me

except hope, how each month
I prayed for a tiny prince
or news that the kingdom
was safe from marauders.
I remember how it felt
that life even for a queen
could be no better.

Here among my sisters I am fearless.
Our men stay blessedly buried
while we hide behind walls,
expecting what will happen
to happen, to soon join them.

Tomorrow: another day

of deja vu and a dead Lord.
At mass I try to sit
by the arched window
in case a sparrow sings.

Guinevere Remembers Modred

Not because I want to
but because he is part of the human lot.
So while the sisters and I pray,
someone is being flogged to death
and God continues.

I do not doubt Arthur slew him
or that the earth took his moldy body
into hell's gut whole,
but at midnight I waken

with his weight on my chest,
the spine of my spirit broken.
If you think two loves cancel one hate
then like a fool you can believe

the past fades, even stays away,
that twelve hours past noon
there shines no darkness.

Sisters in Christ, it is time
for us to gather and sing.
The woman who leads you

knew Satan and gave herself
to two good men.
Bow your heads lest you see
her eyes fill with fire and blood.

Guinevere Remembers His Voice

We had gathered in the Great Hall
to feast on the new knight's return
among hissing torches, lutes,
and a midnight rainstorm.

Everyone's talk clung to the walls
like moss dampening the tapestry
until his bold brass-bell words
showered the court with wit and song.

I turned too, facing the timbre
that shivered the air all motes.
He tipped his head, laughed, the King nodded.
Like mares we waited to hear our names.

In time mine found the trumpet of his mouth
and turned the world to music.
When I became an echo
he left for silence, quest, and Elaine.

Sometimes I still heard it in the garden
or on the winding tower stair
or in a lark's waterfall melody
shaped by the green tree's throat.

Now I hardly recall how to write Regina,
how his chest trembled for love of my hand.
Lord God, is Jesus a baritone
speaker, songster, holy whisper, precious sound?

Even as despair exhausts every prayer
I wait for one more word.
Hark.
      Yes.
            Amen.

Guinevere Remembers the Day of Her Death

like it was yesterday,
one of those long ones early in summer
when night lasts an hour
and all the rest of time
the treeline stays darker than sky.

In the garden I advised a postulant sick
with love. Think of Jesus now,
his pain in our hearts
reminding us we are eternal,
God a small star.

It was windless
with lilies barely nodding at the exchange
of an old woman's doubt
versus human passion.
I am not you, both of us spoke
truth for truth.

The haze became dusk,
bluishness everywhere.
Swallows stayed awake to the faint end.

Alone I lay where I had fallen
crushing grass, chilling dew
with the smell of my skin.
Then the black circle tightened.
I forgot both men before letting go
this ancient name.
Whose kingdom will last forever?
My eyes are open.
I do not blink.

Still Lives

Still Life: Woman with Pear

It is an Egyptian morning,
the woman's porch glazed
with sugar and light,
one pear capable of sustaining the dead
for a thousand years.

D'anjou balances the table
slightly off-center.
The woman admires its shape
so different than the moon,
a revolving delta of speckled gloss
with a crimson medal of valor.

Can her profile remember blossom?
From a world in flux
all that remains is a tomb.
She sits, broad-based,
pointing to heaven above the roof.
Inside are chambers no one has traveled
and four smooth seeds
she will give the pharaoh.

Still Life: Woman with Demon

Suffused by morning light
the woman on the porch
beholds a demon.

He stands on her green glass floor
shaking a stick and berating.
Must have climbed through the crack
between mullion and putty
between honesty and truth
between molding and sill.

She offers a rind of toast
he is in no mood for,
stomping one clawed foot
to protest dust and crumbs.
Rudeness confuses her—the presumption
of his will to join her.

But then a scratchy arm rises
as if to brandish or wave
and the moment clears.
It has been so long since human touch
that she will remain seen with anything:
her face an invitation
her hand an extension
one knee shrinking and bare.

Still Life: Woman with Shadow

There is only one self trapped inside.
So who is the dark other
sharing the porch
with a free woman?

A question mark hovering close.
Perhaps. The sinister shape
of what might have been.
Or a thickening of dust
in pointillist silhouette.

She raises her hand:
it seems to follow.
Ray for ray a cartwheel
astonishes the glass

until as if to steal the moon's ugly face
the sun finds the roof of her head.
Tell me what it is like to be happy.
She pulls the black stole around her
shoulders, pulls the henchman's hood over her
hair, pulls the gypsy swirl up on her
hips, pulls cloister stockings onto her
feet, pulls licorice silk from her
womb to say: Of myself and light I made you.

Still Life: Woman with Vase

The concept involves container.
On morning's porch a woman sits
rocking, changing places with air.
Her feet rest on a peppermint rag rug
like the dog who died last winter.

You have seen this before:
the front of the house enclosing eyesight,
the woman confined by the porch,
a small table drawing sunshine.

To make matters worse
pussy willows cut early March
are forced to remember.
Where she stands is a hothouse
snipping the ends, her children
from before they were born
mindlessly rubbing.

Still Life: Woman with Body

A woman stands on her glass porch
three-sided with morning's light,
a bad day, the purple tree still in her.

She knows about the tree from books
and the blue viaduct glyph
on the back of her hand.
The bag of her body
holds a pint of soul and red weeping.

So she keeps the door shut.
No one knows how she came to possess
this dreadful house, a self
presumed liquid, clearly hers.

Small lever on a dead door.
It resists, she lays down the trowel
with which to keep things in clay pots.
From soil, starlight, spit of creation
bloom motes and violet.

Bloom. The door is just a mouth.
From her smile comes what she was
all along too polite to say:
red fishbowl above the steps,
the dance of Chinese windchimes
shattering cold air.